SEP − 5 2018

SPOTLIGHT ON CIVIC ACTION

CIVIC VIRTUE
HONESTY, MUTUAL RESPECT, AND COOPERATION

GERARD VAN ARK

PowerKiDS press™

NEW YORK

Published in 2018 by The Rosen Publishing Group, Inc.
29 East 21st Street, New York, NY 10010

Editor: Elizabeth Krajnik
Book Design: Michael Flynn
Interior Layout: Rachel Rising

Photo Credits: Cover KidStock/Blend Images/Getty Images; p. 5 Stockr/Shutterstock.com; p. 7 DEA / VENERANDA BIBLIOTECA AMBROSIANA/De Agostini Picture Library/Getty Images; p. 9 fstop123/E+/Shutterstock.com; p. 11 ESB Professional/Shutterstock.com; p. 13 Courtesy of the Library of Congress; pp.13,17, 21, 23 (background) Evgeny Karandaev/Shutterstock.com; p. 15 Kent Sievers/Shutterstock.com; p. 17 New York Daily News Archive/Contributor/ Getty Images; pp.18, 27 iStockphoto.com/asiseeit; pp.19, 29, 30 iStockphoto.com/FatCamera; p. 21 https:// en.wikipedia.org/wiki/United_States_Declaration_of_Independence#/media/File:United_States_Declaration_of_ Independence.jpg; p. 23 https://en.wikipedia.org/wiki/File:Constitution_of_the_United_States,_page_1.jpg; p. 25 @ iStockphoto.com/Image Source; p. 26 iStockphoto.com/kali9.

Cataloging-in-Publication Data

Names: van Ark, Gerard.
Title: Civic virtue: honesty, mutual respect, and cooperation / Gerard van Ark.
Description: New York : PowerKids Press, 2018. | Series: Spotlight on civic action | Includes index.
Identifiers: ISBN 9781538327890 (pbk.) | ISBN 9781508164005 (library bound) | ISBN 9781538328019 (6 pack)
Subjects: LCSH: Social ethics--Juvenile literature. | Social values--Juvenile literature. | Social action--Juvenile literature.
Classification: LCC HM665.V36 2018 | DDC 179/.8--dc23

Manufactured in China

CPSIA Compliance Information: Batch #BW18PK For further information contact Rosen Publishing, New York, New York at 1-800-237-9932.

CONTENTS

CHAPTER ONE

WHAT IS CIVIC VIRTUE?

Civic **virtue** refers to what people can do to keep society running smoothly. By taking part in certain activities, people can work toward the common good. The common good refers to the things citizens do that benefit all—or most—other citizens.

Some experts say that civic virtue can benefit an individual's well-being more than doing things to benefit himself or herself alone. Knowing you've done something to help others is rewarding and makes you feel good.

Doing activities that show your civic virtue builds trust with other citizens who also take part in these activities. Paying income tax, taking part in jury duty, and voting all make an individual a good citizen. If some citizens find out that others don't do these things, they may not trust them as much.

Doing things such as paying taxes benefits all members of society. Taxes pay for **infrastructure** and other public needs.

CHAPTER TWO

THE ROOTS OF CIVIC VIRTUE

The idea of civic virtue can be traced back to 380 BC when Plato, a Greek **philosopher**, wrote *The Republic*. In Plato's *The Republic*, the philosopher Socrates says that courage as a virtue can be found in what an individual learns from the city in which he or she lives. This means that a person can develop the virtue of courage by following that city's laws and customs.

Aristotle, another Greek philosopher, said that people can achieve happiness by having civic and **moral** virtue. He believed that education in these virtues should start in the home.

Thomas Aquinas, a **theologian** and philosopher, believed that the highest good comes from God. He said that the goal of virtue is to achieve happiness. According to Aquinas, imperfect happiness is achievable in this life, but perfect happiness is not.

THOMAS   DE AQVINO

VERITA GV
TEM T
MEDI M
TABI
T

Aquinas believed that we need virtue to achieve happiness.
Virtue helps us understand what happiness truly is.

CHAPTER THREE

CIVIC VIRTUE IN THE EARLY UNITED STATES

Many of the United States' Founding Fathers believed that virtue is necessary for self-government. Unlike Aquinas, many of the founders didn't think virtue necessarily came from closeness to God or religion. Many people who lived at the same time as the Founding Fathers believed that religion helped people govern themselves. While religion may help teach people virtue, people can be virtuous without being religious.

The Founding Fathers believed that civic virtue is necessary for the U.S. Constitution to work. According to Aristotle, virtue is the middle between extremes. Too much or too little of a virtue can have negative results. In order for these virtues to apply, citizens must act on their virtuous thoughts and words and make this action become a habit. By making their actions habits, citizens can show civic virtue and help the government operate smoothly.

We can think and talk about virtuous things such as respect, but respect is only virtuous when we practice it.

CHAPTER FOUR

EXERCISING CIVIC VIRTUE

The Founding Fathers believed the virtues of justice, self-governance, **humility**, responsibility, **perseverance**, courage, respect, contribution, and **integrity** were necessary for U.S. citizens. The United States relies on honesty and trust to function as a progressive nation that values its citizens.

In the United States, there are many different ways people can exercise civic virtue. These ways rely on American citizens being truthful and inclusive. Americans celebrate **unique** national holidays, such as Memorial Day, Independence Day, and Martin Luther King Jr.'s birthday. They vote for the people they believe deserve to hold public office. This includes local officials right up to the vice president and the president. Men and women enlist in the military to protect the nation. Civic virtue focuses on Americans sometimes setting aside their individuality to work toward the good of all citizens.

Volunteering is a good way to show civic virtue. Taking care of the planet is virtuous. Earth belongs to everyone and keeping it clean is beneficial for the present generation and future generations.

CHAPTER FIVE

THE ROLE OF THE INDIVIDUAL

Citizens have certain responsibilities. If everyone practices civic virtue on their own, it benefits all citizens. Think of it this way: if you show others that you have voted, they may go out and vote too.

As is usually the case with civic virtue, it's the individual's choice whether they vote. In the United States, many people fought for all American citizens to have the right to vote. The 15th and 19th Amendments to the U.S. Constitution protect the voting rights of American citizens regardless of race or sex.

The U.S. Constitution also guarantees the protection of other individual rights. However, sometimes even the Constitution can't make sure the U.S. government doesn't get too powerful. By exercising their individual rights, American citizens can help prevent this.

This poster from Nazi Germany says: "Warning. Spies. Be careful when talking!" When Adolf Hitler rose to power in Germany in 1933, he got rid of parts of the German constitution that protected individual freedoms, including freedom of press, speech, and assembly.

CHAPTER SIX

WORKING WITH OTHERS

Americans who exercise their individual rights can help achieve the common good. This idea combines the ideas of classical liberalism, which aims to protect the rights of the individual, and classical republicanism, which promotes the common good as most important. In order to reach this common good, people need to work together and help each other as much as they can.

It may seem as though classical republicanism and classical liberalism are opposites. How can they both exist in one government?

It is true that these are two very different ways of thinking. However, with each generation, Americans try to find new ways to bring them closer together. By joining forces and supporting new laws, citizens can further protect individual rights and the common good. Civic participation helps strengthen the United States and its government.

WARNING

NEIGHBORHOOD
WATCH
PROTECTED AREA

There are two main types of civic participation: social action and political action. Neighbors can join together to create a neighborhood watch, which is a type of social action. Political action requires citizens to meet and work with political officials to solve social problems.

CHAPTER SEVEN

BEING HONEST

One of the fundamental parts of civic virtue is honesty. The success of the U.S. model of government depends on honesty from the people, whether they are politicians or regular citizens. Being honest will help your peers trust you, and building trust promotes the common good.

In the world of politics, honesty is especially important. When politicians are very clear about what their **intentions** are and how they would like to lead, it makes it easier for people to decide whether they agree with them. If a politician lies about something, it can make people feel uneasy and distrust the politician.

An example of dishonesty causing political distrust is President Richard Nixon's role in the Watergate **scandal** in the 1970s. President Nixon wasn't truthful about what he did. As a result, he faced **impeachment**. He resigned from the presidency in 1974.

DAILY NEWS
NEW YORK'S PICTURE NEWSPAPER ®

15¢

Vol. 56. No. 39 · Copr. 1974 New York News Inc. · New York, N.Y. 10017, Friday, August 9, 1974★ · WEATHER: Partly cloudy, windy and mild.

NIXON RESIGNS

Acts in 'Interest of Nation,' Asks for End to Bitterness

Ford Will Take Oath at Noon, Kissinger Agrees to Stay On

Special 8-Page Pullout; Stories Start on Page 2

Being honest is always a good thing. Some Americans don't trust the U.S. government because of incidents like the Watergate scandal.

CHAPTER EIGHT

RESPECTING YOUR PEERS

In the United States, there should be a balance of citizens' respect for the government and the government's respect for American citizens. Without this balance, the constitutional democracy on which the nation is founded could fall apart. The government must respect the fact that there are limits to its power.

Everyone has worth, and everyone deserves respect. Make sure you're treating your peers respectfully. This can help make your community—and the entire country—a nicer place to live.

In a similar way, American citizens must respect the Constitution and what it stands for. The U.S. Constitution makes our form of government possible. American citizens must also respect other citizens' rights. All citizens should be equal under the Constitution. It's important to respect this idea.

You might not agree with people's choices all the time, but you must respect the fact that they have the ability to make their own choices.

CHAPTER NINE

THE LIBERAL TRADITION

Classical liberalism refers to the political ideal that focuses on protecting and **enhancing** the freedom of individual citizens. A government is required to protect individual rights but can also threaten individual rights. In the United States, the government has been created in a way that aims to protect citizens' individual rights and prevent officials from **abusing** their power. The ideas of classical liberalism originated in the 17th century and were further developed throughout the Enlightenment period of the 18th century.

The liberal tradition suggests that the government should do everything in its power to make sure individuals can live as freely as possible. This means that everyone should have the same rights, the same opportunities, and the same benefits. In the United States, the people created the government to best suit their needs and the government gets its power from the people.

The Declaration of Independence is one example of a document that promotes the ideas of classical liberalism.

CHAPTER TEN

THE REPUBLICAN TRADITION

Classical republicanism refers to the political ideal that focuses on the promotion of the common good. The common good, according to republicanism, is the main purpose of government. In order to promote the common good, citizens must exercise their civic virtue and stay informed about or participate in politics. They must be aware of any abuses of power within the government.

In the United States, classical republicanism requires citizens to respect the Constitution and its principles and understand that it is beneficial to show civic virtue. Classical republicanism comes from the word "republic." A republic is a country that is governed by elected representatives and by an elected leader rather than by a king or a queen. The United States is a republic.

The U.S. Constitution is a good example of a document that reflects many ideas associated with classical republicanism.

The preamble of the U.S. Constitution guarantees Americans a republican government. This means the government will be guided by the ideals of classical republicanism.

CHAPTER ELEVEN

CIVIC VIRTUE IN ACTION

Civic virtue and political participation are instrumental in maintaining the United States' republican form of government. Civic virtue requires citizens to think of the common good and actively work toward it. In order for the U.S. government to operate properly, all capable citizens should contribute their time and efforts. This works toward the common good.

In the United States, showing civic virtue could be something as small as paying a parking ticket or something as large as serving as a juror on an important criminal case. A great way to show civic virtue is to help out at school when you're asked to do so. This shows that you are respectful and willing to cooperate. People who show civic virtue keep the country running. This trait is needed to bring citizens together.

Jury service is just one way ordinary citizens can show civic virtue. Jurors are selected from different backgrounds to provide impartial viewpoints during court cases.

CHAPTER TWELVE

HOW TO SHOW CIVIC VIRTUE

In the United States, citizens are governed by the rule of law. This means there are laws and widely accepted rules that govern all citizens, including people in positions of authority such as the president and police officers. The laws may limit people's actions to protect other citizens' rights and promote the common good.

Police officers are supposed to follow the rule of law just like everyone else. They're supposed to protect citizens' rights and promote the common good.

A good way to show civic virtue is to make sure you're following laws and rules in your daily life. Maybe you make sure you're putting recyclable items in the correct bin rather than throwing them out. Or perhaps it means you help a classmate understand a topic so they can participate in class discussion. These things benefit you and others, which is the basis of civic virtue.

CHAPTER THIRTEEN

WHY CIVIC VIRTUE IS IMPORTANT

Showing civic virtue can make you and other citizens happier and freer. By following the rule of law and actively participating in politics and your community, you are working toward the common good. Although following rules and laws might seem boring, it can actually make citizens feel as though they have more of an equal opportunity in society.

Imagine if schools, public buildings, and workplaces were still **segregated** despite the Civil Rights Act of 1964. African Americans wouldn't be able to obtain the same education, the same jobs, or the same housing as white people. Today, many African Americans and other minority groups feel they still have an unequal chance in life.

Each citizen's participation in politics and their community is crucial to the success of the U.S. government. If no one participates, the U.S. government could turn into a monarchy or a dictatorship.

Citizens whose individual rights aren't threatened are more likely to feel happy. Happier citizens tend to be more active in the government at the local, state, and federal levels.

CHAPTER FOURTEEN

GET INVOLVED!

No government is perfect. It is your job as a citizen to recognize issues in the government that negatively affect other citizens' lives and work toward fixing these issues. Even though you may be too young to vote in elections, you can start practicing civic virtue now.

You can be an active participant in your community. You can get involved in a number of ways. Volunteering your time is a great way to work toward the common good. You could volunteer to help build houses for the homeless or help plant a community garden that gives food to the hungry.

If you notice something wrong in your community, you can work to fix it. Civic virtue means working to make things better for everyone.

GLOSSARY

abuse (uh-BYOOS) To treat or use something in a wrong or unfair way; also, the act of doing so.

enhance (in-HANS) To make greater or better.

humility (hyoo-MIH-luh-tee) The quality of being humble.

impeachment (im-PEECH-muhnt) The act of charging a public official with a crime done while in office.

infrastructure (IN-fruh-struhk-shur) The equipment and structures needed for a country, state, or region to function properly.

integrity (in-TEH-gruh-tee) The quality of being fair and honest.

intention (in-TEN-shun) An aim or plan.

moral (MOR-uhl) Concerned with or relating to what is right and wrong in human behavior.

perseverance (puhr-suh-VEER-uhns) The quality that allows someone to continue to do something even though it is difficult.

philosopher (fuh-LAH-suh-fuhr) A person who tries to discover and to understand the basic nature of knowledge.

scandal (SKAN-duhl) Conduct that people find shocking and bad.

segregated (SEH-grih-gay-ted) Set apart from others because of their race, religion, gender, or class.

theologian (thee-uh-LOW-juhn) A person who is an expert on theology, or the study and explanation of religious faith, practice, and experience.

unique (yoo-NEEK) Special or different from anything else.

virtue (VUHR-chyoo) Morally good behavior or character.

INDEX

PRIMARY SOURCE LIST

Page 13
Propaganda poster showing a man pretending to read a newspaper as he eavesdrops on two men who are talking. Theo Matejko. 1939. Created in Berlin, Germany. Published by Wilhelm Limpert. Now kept at the Library of Congress Prints and Photographs Division Washington, D.C.

Page 21
Engrossed Declaration of Independence. Created in 1776. Now kept at the National Archives Washington, D.C.

Page 23
Constitution of the United States. Created in 1787. Now kept at the National Archives Washington, D.C.

WEBSITES

Due to the changing nature of Internet links, PowerKids Press has developed an online list of websites related to the subject of this book. This site is updated regularly. Please use this link to access the list: www.powerkidslinks.com/sociv/coop